Song of the Cid & Other Poems by William Lisle Bowles

William Lisle Bowles was born on 24th September 1762 at King's Sutton in Northamptonshire.

His great-grandfather, grandfather and his father, William Thomas Bowles, had all been parish priests and inevitably Bowles would join their line.

In 1789 Bowles published, a small quarto volume, Fourteen Sonnets, which was received with extraordinary praise, not only by the general public, but by such revered poets as Samuel Taylor Coleridge and Wordsworth.

After receiving his degree at Oxford, Bowles now began his career in service to the Church of England.

His years of service perhaps diminished both his stature as a poet and certainly the way he was viewed. For much of his career Bowles was seen as rather soft when set against his contemporaries but in the end his ability as a poet was enshrined, after a long and ferocious attack against him, by the principles he so eloquently wrote about and adhered too.

In personality and nature Bowles was said to be an amiable, absent-minded, but rather eccentric man. His poems speak warmly of a refinement of feeling, tenderness, and pensive thought, but are lacking in power and passion. But that should not diminish their value or appreciation to us.

Bowles maintained that images drawn from nature are poetically finer than those drawn from art; and that in the highest kinds of poetry the themes or passions handled should be of the general or elemental kind, and not the transient manners of any society.

As well as his poetry Bowles was also responsible for writing a Life of Bishop Ken (in two volumes, 1830–1831), Coombe Ellen and St. Michael's Mount (1798), The Battle of the Nile (1799), and The Sorrows of Switzerland (1801).

William Lisle Bowles died on April 7th, 1850 at the age of 87.

Index of Contents
Song of the Cid
The Sanctuary: a Dramatic Sketch
Scene I
Scene II
Scene III
Childe Harold's Last Pilgrimage
The Egyptian Tomb
Chantrey's Sleeping Children
On Miss Fitzgerald and Lord Kerry Planting two Cedars in the Churchyard of Bremhill
The Greenwich Pensioners
Glastonbury Abbey and Wells Cathedral

Silchester, the Ancient Caleva
Restoration of Malmesbury Abbey
On the Funeral of Charles the First, at Night, in St George's Chapel, Windsor
On Seeing Plants in the Windows of Seth Ward's College
Morley's Farewell to the Cottage of Isaak Walton
The Grave of Bishop Ken
The Legend of St Cecilia and the Angel
Supposed Address to Bishop Ken
On an Eclipse of the Moon at Midnight
To Lady Valletort
On Seeing a Bust of R. B. Sheridan
Return of George III to Windsor Castle
On Meeting some Friends of Youth at Cheltenham
The Lay of Talbot the Troubadour: a Legend of Lacock Abbey
The Ark: a Poem for Music
Written after the Consecration of the New Church at Kingswood
On the Death of Dr Burgess, the late Bishop of Salisbury
Lines written on Fonthill Abbey
Epitaph on Benjamin Tremlyn, an Old Soldier, buried in Bremhill Churchyard
Epitaph on Robert Southey
Sonnet, written in a copy of Falconer's "Shipwreck"
On first Hearing Caradori Sing
Salisbury Cathedral
Lockswell
On Mozart
Epitaph on John Harding, in the Churchyard of Bremhill
On the Death of William Linley, Esq.
Inscribed to the Marchioness of Lansdowne
Hymn for Music, after the Battle of Waterloo
Inscriptions in the Gardens of Bremhill Rectory:—
On a Tree commanding a view of the whole extent of Bowood
On a Rural Seat
On the Front of a Hermitage, near a Dial
Quieti et Musis

SONG OF THE CID

The Cid is sitting, in martial state,
Within Valencia's wall;
And chiefs of high renown attend
The knightly festival.

Brave Alvar Fanez, and a troop
Of gallant men, were there;
And there came Donna Ximena,
His wife and daughters fair.

When the footpage bent on his knee,
What tidings brought he then?
Morocco's king is on the seas,
With fifty thousand men.

Now God be praised! the Cid he cried,
Let every hold be stored:
Let fly the holy Gonfalon,
And give, "St James," the word.

And now, upon the turret high,
Was heard the signal drum;
And loud the watchman blew his trump,
And cried, They come! they come!

The Cid then raised his sword on high,
And by God's Mother swore,
These walls, hard-gotten, he would keep,
Or bathe their base in gore.

My wife, my daughter, what, in tears!
Nay, hang not thus your head;
For you shall see how well we fight;
How soldiers earn their bread.

We will go out against the Moors,
And crush them in your sight;
And all the Christians shouted loud,
May God defend the right!

He took his wife and daughter's hand,
So resolute was he,
And led them to the highest tower
That overlooks the sea.

They saw how vast a pagan power
Came sailing o'er the brine;
They saw, beneath the morning light,
The Moorish crescents shine.

These ladies then grew deadly pale,
As heart-struck with dismay;
And when they heard the tambours beat,
They turned their heads away.

The thronged streamers glittering flew,
The sun was shining bright,

Now cheer, the valiant Cid he cried,
This is a glorious sight!

Whilst thus, with shuddering look aghast,
These fearful ladies stood,
The Cid, he raised his sword, and cried,
All this is for your good:

Ere fifteen days are gone and past,
If God assist the right,
Those tambours that now sound to scare,
Shall sound for your delight.

The Moors who pressed beneath the towers,
Now Allah! Allah! sung;
Each Christian knight his broadsword drew,
And loud the trumpets rung.

Then up, the noble Cid bespoke,
Let each brave warrior go,
And arm himself, in dusk of morn,
Ere chanticleer shall crow;

And in the lofty minster church,
On Santiago call,—
That good Bishop Hieronymo,
Shall there absolve you all.

But let us prudent counsel take,
In this eventful hour;
For yon proud infidels, I ween,
They are a mighty power.

Then AlvarFanez counselled well,
I, noble Cid, will go,
And ambush with three hundred men,
Ere the first cock doth crow:

And when against the Moorish men
You, Cid, lead on your powers,
We, dauntless, on the other side
Will fall on them with ours.

This counsel pleased the Chieftain well:
He said, it should be so;
And the good Bishop should sing mass,
Ere the first cock did crow.

The day is gone, the night is come;
At cock-crow all appear,
In Pedro's church to shrive themselves,
And holy mass to hear:

On Santiago there they called,
To hear them and to save;
And that good Bishop, at the mass,
Great absolution gave.

Fear not, he cried, when thousands bleed,
When horse on man shall roll!
Whoever dies, I take his sins,
And God be with his soul.

A boon! a boon! the Bishop cried,
I have sung mass to-day;
Let me the brunt of battle bear,
Cid, in the bloody fray.

Now AlvarFanez and his men
Had gained the thicket's shade;
And, with hushed breath and anxious eye,
Had there their ambush laid.

Four thousand men, in glittering arms,
All issued from the gate;
Whilst the bold Cid, before them all,
On Bavieca sate.

They passed the ambush on the left,
And marched o'er dale and down,
Till soon they got the Moorish camp
Betwixt them and the town.

The Cid then spurred his horse, and set
The battle in array.
Pero Bermudez proudly bore
His standard on that day.

When this the Moors astonied saw,
Allah! began their cry:
The tambours beat, the cymbals rung,
As they would rend the sky.

Banner, advance! the Cid he cried,
And raised aloft his sword:
And all the host set up the shout,

St Mary and our Lord!

That good Bishop Hieronymo,
Bravely his battle bore;
And shouted, as he spurred his steed,
For bold Campeador!

The Moorish and the Christian host
Now mix their dying cries;
And many a horse along the plain,
Without his rider flies.

Now sinks the Crescent, now the Cross,
As the fierce hosts assail;
But what against o'erwhelming might
Can valour'sself avail?

Campeador, all bathed in blood,
Spurred on his horse amain;
And, Santiago! cried aloud,
For Bivar and for Spain!

Now Alvar Fanez and his men,
Who crouched in thickets low,
Leaped up, and, with the lightning glance,
Rushed, shouting, on the foe.

The Moors, who saw their pennons gay
All waving in the wind,
Fled in dismay, for still they feared,
A greater host behind.

The Crescent falls. Pursue! pursue!
Haste—spur along the plain!
See where they sink—see where they lie,
The fainting and the slain!

Of fifty thousand, who at morn
Came forth in armour bright,
Scarce fifteen thousand souls were left,
To tell the tale at night.

The Cid then wiped his bloody brow,
And thus was heard to say:
Well, Bavieca, hast thou sped,
My noble horse, to-day!

If thousands then escaped the sword,

Let none the Cid condemn;
For they were swept into the sea,
And the surge went over them.

There's many a maid of Tetuan,
All day shall sit and weep,
But never see her lover's sail
Shine on the northern deep.

There's many a mother, with her babe,
Shall pace the sounding shore,
And think upon its father's smile,
Whom she shall see no more.

Rock, hoary ocean, mournfully,
Upon thy billowy bed;
For, dark and deep, thy surges sweep,
O'er thousands of the dead.

FOOTNOTES

Footnote : This ballad was written to be introduced in "The Missionary," but was omitted, as calculated to distract attention from the leading incidents of the story. It has, indeed, no connexion whatever with the poem.

Footnote : Banner consecrated by the Pope.

THE SANCTUARY

A DRAMATIC SKETCH

In this wise the Duke of Gloucester took upon himself the order and governance of the young King, whom, with much honour and humble reverence, he conveyed towards London. But the tidings of this matter came hastily to the Queen, a little before the midnight following; and that, in secret wise, her son was taken, her brother and other friends arrested, and sent no man wist whither, to be done with God wot what. With which tidings the Queen, with great heaviness, bewailed her child's reign, her friend's mischance, and her own misfortune, damning the time that ever she dissuaded the gathering of powers about the King; got herself, in all haste possible, with her young son and her daughter, out of the palace of Westminster, in which they then lay, into the Sanctuary; lodging herself and company there in the Abbott's place.—Speed's "History of England," book ix.

SCENE I

ELIZABETH, widow of Edward IV., in the palace of Westminster, watching her youngest son, RCHARD, sleeping.

ELIZABETH
The minster-clock tolls midnight; I have watched
Night after night, and heard the same sad sound
Knolling; the same sad sound, night after night;
As if, amid the world's deep silence, Time,
Pausing a moment in his onward flight,
From yonder solitary, moonlit pile,
More awful spoke, as with a voice from heaven,
Of days and hours departed, and of those
That "are not;" till, like dreams of yesterday,
The very echo dies!
Oh, my poor child!
Thou hast been long asleep; by the pale lamp
I sit and watch thy slumbers; thy calm lids
Are closed; thy lips just parted; one hand lies
Upon thy breast, that scarce is seen to heave
Beneath it; and thy breath so still is drawn,
Save to a sleepless mother's listening ear,
It were inaudible; and, see! a smile
Seems even now lighting on thy lip, dear boy,
As thou wert dreaming of delightful things
In some celestial region of sweet sounds,
Or summer fields, and skies without a cloud;
(Ah! how unlike this dark and troubled world!)
Let not one kiss awaken thee, one kiss,
Mingled with tears and prayer to God in heaven.
So dream; and never, never may those eyes
Awake suffused with tears, as mine are now,
To think that life's best hopes are such a dream!
Now sleeps the city through its vast extent,
That, restless as the ocean-waves, at morn,
With its ten thousand voices shall awake,
Lifting the murmur of its multitude
To heaven's still gate! Now all is hushed as death;
None are awake, save those who wake to weep,
Like me; save those who meditate revenge,
Or beckon muttering Murder. God of heaven!
From the hyena panting for their blood,
Oh save my youthful Edward! and, poor child!
Preserve thy innocence to happier hours.
Hark! There is knocking at the western gate.

A messenger enters, and announces to her that her brother had been arrested on the road, by the Duke of Glo'ster.

ELIZABETH
O my poor child, thou sleepest now in peace!
Wilt thou sleep thus another year? shall I
Hang o'er thee with a mother's look of love,
Thus bend beside thy bed, thus part the hair
Upon thy forehead, and thus kiss thy cheek?
Richard, awake! the tiger is abroad.
We must to sanctuary instantly.

RICHARD awaking.

RICHARD
Oh! I have had the sweetest dreams, dear mother!
Methought my brother Edward and myself
And—

ELIZABETH
Come, these are no times to talk of dreams;
We must to sanctuary, my poor boy;
We'll talk of dreams hereafter. Kneel with me.

Takes him from his couch, and kisses him.

RICHARD
Mother, why do you weep and tremble so?

ELIZABETH
I have a pain at heart! Come, stir thee, boy!
Lift up thy innocent hands to Heaven; here kneel
And pray with me before this crucifix.

Her daughters enter, and they all kneel together.

SCENE II

The Sanctuary at Westminster.

RICHARD
O my dear mother! why do we sit here,
Amid these dusky walls and arches dim,
When it is summer in the fields without,
And sunshine? Say, is not my brother king,
Why will he not come here to play with me;
Shall I not see my brother?

ELIZABETH
My own child,

Oh! let me hide these tears upon thy head!
Thy brother, shalt thou see him? Yes, I hope.
Come, I will tell a tale:—There was a boy
Who had a cruel uncle—

RICHARD
I have heard
My uncle Glo'ster was a cruel man;
But he was always kind to me, and said
That I should be a king, if Edward died;
I'd rather be a bird to fly away,
Or sing—

ELIZABETH
The serpent's eye of fire,
With slow and deadly glare, poor bird, I fear,
Is fixed on thee and Edward—God avert it!

RICHARD
And therefore must not I go out to play?

ELIZABETH
Go, play among the tombs—I will go too;
Go, play with skulls and bones; or see the train
Of sceptred kings come slowly through the gloom,
And widowed queens move in the shroud of death
Along the glimmering aisles and hollow vaults.
Would I were with them—I shall be so soon!

RICHARD
Mother, methought I saw him yesterday—

ELIZABETH
Saw whom?

RICHARD
My father; and he seemed to look—
I cannot say how sadly. Could it be
His spirit? He was armed, but very pale
And sorrowful his countenance. I heard
No sound of footsteps when he moved away
And disappeared among the distant tombs
In further darkness.

ELIZABETH
O my son, my son!
Thou hadst a king thy father—he is dead;
Thou hadst been happier as a peasant's child!

RICHARD
Oh! how I wish I were a shepherd's boy,
For then, dear mother! I would run and play
With Edward; and we two, in primrose-time,
Would wander out among the villages,
Or go a-Maying by some river's side,
And mark the minnow-shoals, when morning shone
Upon the yellow gravel, shoot away
Beneath the old gray arch, or bring home cowslips
For all my sisters, for Elizabeth,
And you, dear mother, if you would not weep so.

ELIZABETH
Richard, break not my heart; give me your hand,
And kneel with me by this cold monument.
Spirit of my loved husband, now in heaven,
If, at this moment, thou dost see thy son,
And me, thus broken-hearted,—oh! if aught
Yet human touches thee, assist these prayers,
That him, and me, and my poor family,
God, in the hour of peril, may protect!
Let not my heart yet break.
Come, my poor boy!

SCENE III

The Cardinal of York—Queen—Richard.

ELIZABETH
Now, my Lord Cardinal, what is the will
Of our great lords with me? Your Grace well knows
I am a helpless woman, have no power;
My only wish, for what of life remains,
Prayer and repose, and for my poor child here
Safety.

CARDINAL
The Council, madam, wish no less;
But, for your son, they deem his durance here
Breeds ill report. This separation, too,
Of those in blood allied, almost of years
The same, who have been cradled in one lap,
What can it say, but that one brother stands
In peril of the other? And, besides,
Were it not for the comfort of them both

That they should be together? Sport, not care,
Becomes their early years.

ELIZABETH
I say not nay;
It is most fitting that my youngest son
Were with the king, his brother; in good faith,
I know it would be comfort to them both:
But, when I think upon the tender years,
Even of the eldest, I must also think
A mother's custody were best for either.
You have no children, else I would not ask,
Is there a guardian like a mother's love?
Richard, look up! This good man here intends
No harm to me or you. Look up, my boy!
No power on earth, nothing but death itself
Shall sever us.
What would you more, my Lord?

CARDINAL
Madam, no man contendeth that your Grace
Is not the fittest guardian of your child,
And tenderest; but, if so it pleases you
Here to lie hid, shut out from all the world,
Be it for humour or for jealousy,
We hold it meetest, that no power on earth
Should so detain a brother of the King.
And let me add, when reasons of the state
Required the absence of your eldest son,
Yourself were well content.

ELIZABETH
Not very well;
Nor is the case the same; one was in health,
The other here declines; and let me marvel
That he, the Lord Protector of this realm,
Should wish him out; for, should aught ill betide,
Suspicion, in some tempers, might arise
Against the keeping of his Grace. My Lord,
Do they complain that my child Richard here
Is with his desolate and widowed mother,
Who has no other comfort? Do they claim
His presence, for that here his residence
Consorts not with his fortunes? I am fixed
Not to come forth and jeopardy his life.

CARDINAL
Jeopardy! Where, and how;—why should, indeed,

Your friends have any fears? Can you say why?

ELIZABETH
Truly; nor why in prison they should be,
As now they are, I know no reason why.
But this I know, that they who, without colour,
Have cast them into prison, if they will,
Their deaths may compass with as little cause.
My Lord, no more of this.

CARDINAL
My gracious queen,
This only let me say; if, by arrest,
Your Grace's high and honourable kin
Be now confined, when trial has been had,
They shall do well; and for your Grace's self,
There never was, nor can be, jeopardy.

ELIZABETH
Why should I trust? That I am innocent!
And were they guilty? That I am more loved,
Even by those enemies, who only hate
Them for my sake!
Therefore I will not forth,
Nor shall my son,—here will we both abide.
These shrines shall be the world to him and me;
These monuments our sad companions;
Or when, as now, the morning sunshine streams
Slant from the rich-hued window's height, and rests
On yonder tomb, it shall discourse to me
Of the brief sunshine in the gloom of life.
No, of heaven's light upon the silent grave;
Of the tired traveller's eternal home;
Of hope and joy beyond this vale of tears.

CARDINAL
Then pardon me. We will not bandy words
Further. If it shall please you, generous queen,
To yield your son, I pledge my life and soul,
Not only for a surety, but estate.
If resolutely still you answer no,
We shall forthwith depart, for nevermore
Will I be suitor in this business
Unto your Majesty, who thus accuse,
Either of want of knowledge or of truth,
Those who would stake their lives on the event.
Madam, farewell!

ELIZABETH (after a pause)
Stay, let me think again.
If you say sooth—and I have found you ever,
My Lord, a faithful friend and counsellor—
Into your hands I here resign, in trust,
My dearest treasure upon earth, my son.
Of you I will require him, before Heaven;
Yet, for the love which his dead father bore you,
For kindnesses of old, and for that trust
The king, my husband, ever placed in you,
Think, if a wretched mother fear too much,
Oh think, and be you wary, lest you fear
Too little!
My poor child, here then we part!
Richard! Almighty God shower on your head
His blessings, when your mother is no more.
Farewell, my own sweet son! Yet, ere we part,
Kiss me again, God only knows, poor babe,
Whether in this world we shall meet again!
Nay, my boy Richard, let me dry thy tears,
Or hide them in my bosom; dearest child,
God's blessing rest with thee!—farewell, farewell!
My heart is almost broken—oh, farewell!

CHILDE HAROLD'S LAST PILGRIMAGE

So ends Childe Harold his last pilgrimage!
Above the Malian surge he stood, and cried,
Liberty! and the shores, from age to age
Renowned, and Sparta's woods and rocks, replied,
Liberty! But a spectre at his side
Stood mocking, and its dart uplifting high
Smote him; he sank to earth in life's fair pride:
Sparta! thy rocks echoed another cry,
And old Ilissus sighed, Die, generous exile, die!

I will not ask sad pity to deplore
His wayward errors, who thus early died;
Still less, Childe Harold, now thou art no more,
Will I say aught of genius misapplied;
Of the past shadows of thy spleen or pride.
But I will bid the Arcadian cypress wave,
Pluck the green laurel from Peneus' side,
And pray thy spirit may such quiet have,
That not one thought unkind be murmured o'er thy grave.

So ends Childe Harold his last pilgrimage!
Ends in that region, in that land renowned,
Whose mighty genius lives in Glory's page,
And on the Muses' consecrated ground;
His pale cheek fading where his brows were bound
With their unfading wreath! I will not call
The nymphs from Pindus' piny shades profound,
But strew some flowers upon thy sable pall,
And follow to the grave a Briton's funeral.

Slow move the plumed hearse, the mourning train,
I mark the long procession with a sigh,
Silently passing to that village fane
Where, Harold, thy forefathers mouldering lie;
Where sleeps the mother, who with tearful eye
Pondering the fortunes of thy onward road,
Hung o'er the slumbers of thine infancy;
Who here, released from every human load,
Receives her long-lost child to the same calm abode.

Bursting Death's silence, could that mother speak,
When first the earth is heaped upon thy head,
In thrilling, but with hollow accent weak,
She thus might give the welcome of the dead:
Here rest, my son, with me—the dream is fled—
The motley mask and the great coil are o'er;
Welcome to me, and to this wormy bed,
Where deep forgetfulness succeeds the roar
Of earth, and fretting passions waste the heart no more.

Here rest!—on all thy wanderings peace repose,
After the fever of thy toilsome way;
No interruption this long silence knows;
Here no vain phantoms lead the soul astray;
The earth-worm feeds on his unconscious prey:
Here both shall sleep in peace till earth and sea
Give up their dead, at that last awful day,
King, Lord, Almighty Judge! remember me;
And may Heaven's mercy rest, my erring child, on thee!

THE EGYPTIAN TOMB

Pomp of Egypt's elder day,
Shade of the mighty passed away,
Whose giant works still frown sublime
'Mid the twilight shades of Time;

Fanes, of sculpture vast and rude,
That strew the sandy solitude,
Lo! before our startled eyes,
As at a wizard's wand, ye rise,
Glimmering larger through the gloom!
While on the secrets of the tomb,
Rapt in other times, we gaze,
The Mother Queen of ancient days,
Her mystic symbol in her hand,
Great Isis, seems herself to stand.

From mazy vaults, high-arched and dim,
Hark! heard ye not Osiris' hymn?
And saw ye not in order dread
The long procession of the dead?
Forms that the night of years concealed,
As by a flash, are here revealed;
Chiefs who sang the victor song;
Sceptredkings,—a shadowy throng,—
From slumber of three thousand years
Each, as in light and life, appears,
Stern as of yore! Yes, vision vast,
Three thousand years have silent passed,
Suns of empire risen and set,
Whose story Time can ne'er forget,
Time, in the morning of her pride
Immense, along the Nile's green side,
The City of the Sun appeared,
And her gigantic image reared.

As Memnon, like a trembling string
When the sun, with rising ray,
Streaked the lonely desert gray,
Sent forth its magic murmuring,
That just was heard,—then died away;
So passed, O Thebes! thy morning pride!
Thy glory was the sound that died!
Dark city of the desolate,
Once thou wert rich, and proud, and great!
This busy-peopled isle was then
A waste, or roamed by savage men
Whose gay descendants now appear
To mark thy wreck of glory here.

Phantom of that city old,
Whose mystic spoils I now behold,
A kingdom's sepulchre, oh say,
Shall Albion's own illustrious day,

Thus darkly close! Her power, her fame
Thus pass away, a shade, a name!
The Mausoleum murmured as I spoke;
A spectre seemed to rise, like towering smoke;
It answered not, but pointed as it fled
To the black carcase of the sightless dead.
Once more I heard the sounds of earthly strife,
And the streets ringing to the stir of life.

CHANTREY'S SLEEPING CHILDREN

Look at those sleeping children; softly tread,
Lest thou do mar their dream, and come not nigh
Till their fond mother, with a kiss, shall cry,
'Tis morn, awake! awake! Ah! they are dead!
Yet folded in each other's arms they lie,
So still—oh, look! so still and smilingly,
So breathing and so beautiful, they seem,
As if to die in youth were but to dream
Of spring and flowers! Of flowers? Yet nearer stand—
There is a lily in one little hand,
Broken, but not faded yet,
As if its cup with tears were wet.
So sleeps that child, not faded, though in death,
And seeming still to hear her sister's breath,
As when she first did lay her head to rest
Gently on that sister's breast,
And kissed her ere she fell asleep!
The archangel's trump alone shall wake that slumber deep.
Take up those flowers that fell
From the dead hand, and sigh a long farewell!
Your spirits rest in bliss!
Yet ere with parting prayers we say,
Farewell for ever to the insensate clay,
Poor maid, those pale lips we will kiss!
Ah! 'tis cold marble! Artist, who hast wrought
This work of nature, feeling, and of thought;
Thine, Chantrey, be the fame
That joins to immortality thy name.
For these sweet children that so sculptured rest—
A sister's head upon a sister's breast—
Age after age shall pass away,
Nor shall their beauty fade, their forms decay.
For here is no corruption; the cold worm
Can never prey upon that beauteous form:
This smile of death that fades not, shall engage

The deep affections of each distant age!
Mothers, till ruin the round world hath rent,
Shall gaze with tears upon the monument!
And fathers sigh, with half-suspended breath:
How sweetly sleep the innocent in death!

July.

ON MISS FITZGERALD AND LORD KERRY PLANTING TWO CEDARS IN THE CHURCHYARD OF BREMHILL

Yes, Pamela, this infant tree
Planted in sacred earth by thee,
Shall strike its root, and pleasant grow
Whilst I am mouldering dust below.
This churchyard turf shall still be green,
When other pastors here are seen,
Who, gazing on that dial gray,
Shall mourn, like me, life's passing ray.
What says its monitory shade?
Thyself so blooming, now shalt fade;
And even that fair and lightsome boy,
Elastic as the step of joy,
The future lord of yon domain,
And all this wide extended plain,
Shall yield to creeping time, when they
Who loved him shall have passed away.
Yet, planted by his youthful hand,
The fellow-cedar still shall stand,
And when it spreads its boughs around,
Shading the consecrated ground,
He may behold its shade, and say
(Himself then haply growing gray),
Yes, I remember, aged tree,
When I was young who planted thee!
But long may time, blithe maiden, spare
Thy beaming eyes and crisped hair,
Thy unaffected converse kind,
Thy gentle and ingenuous mind.
For him when I in dust repose,
May virtue guide him as he grows;
And may he, when no longer young,
Resemble those from whom he sprung!
Then let these trees extend their shade,
Or live or die, or bloom or fade,
Virtue, uninjured and sublime,
Shall lift her brightest wreath, untouched by time.

THE GREENWICH PENSIONERS

When evening listened to the dipping oar,
Forgetting the loud city's ceaseless roar,
By the green banks, where Thames, with conscious pride,
Reflects that stately structure on his side,

Within whose walls, as their long labours close,
The wanderers of the ocean find repose,
We wore, in social ease, the hours away,
The passing visit of a summer's day.

Whilst some to range the breezy hill are gone,
I lingered on the river's marge alone,
Mingled with groups of ancient sailors gray,
And watched the last bright sunshine steal away.

As thus I mused amidst the various train
Of toil-worn wanderers of the perilous main,
Two sailors,—well I marked them, as the beam
Of parting day yet lingered on the stream,
And the sun sank behind the shady reach,—
Hastened with tottering footsteps to the beach.

The one had lost a limb in Nile's dread fight;
Total eclipse had veiled the other's sight,
For ever. As I drew, more anxious, near,
I stood intent, if they should speak, to hear;
But neither said a word. He who was blind,
Stood as to feel the comfortable wind,
That gently lifted his gray hair—his face
Seemed then of a faint smile to wear the trace.

The other fixed his gaze upon the light,
Parting, and when the sun had vanished quite,
Methought a starting tear that Heaven might bless,
Unfelt, or felt with transient tenderness,
Came to his aged eyes, and touched his cheek!
And then, as meek and silent as before,
Back, hand in hand, they went, and left the shore.

As they departed through the unheeding crowd,
A caged bird sang from the casement loud,
And then I heard alone that blind man say,
The music of the bird is sweet to-day!

I said, O heavenly Father! none may know
The cause these have for silence or for woe!
Here they appeared heartstricken and resigned
Amidst the unheeding tumult of mankind.

There is a world, a pure unclouded clime,
Where there is neither grief, nor death, nor time,
Nor loss of friends! Perhaps when yonder bell
Pealed slow, and bade the dying day farewell,
Ere yet the glimmering landscape sank to night,
They thought upon that world of distant light!
And when the blind man, lifting light his hair,
Felt the faint wind, he raised a warmer prayer;
Then sighed, as the blithe bird sang o'er his head,
No morn shall shine on me till I am dead!

GLASTONBURY ABBEY AND WELLS CATHEDRAL

WRITTEN AFTER VIEWING THE RUINS OF THE ONE, AND HEARING THE CHURCH SERVICE IN THE OTHER

Glory and boast of Avalon's fair vale,
How beautiful thy ancient turrets rose!
Fancy yet sees them, in the sunshine pale,
Gleaming, or, more majestic, in repose,
When, west-away, the crimson landscape glows,
Casting their shadows on the waters wide.
How sweet the sounds, that, at still day-light's close,
Came blended with the airs of eventide,
When through the glimmering aisle faint "Misereres" died!

But all is silent now! silent the bell,
That, heard from yonder ivied turret high,
Warned the cowled brother from his midnight cell;
Silent the vesper-chant, the litany
Responsive to the organ!—scattered lie
The wrecks of the proud pile, 'mid arches gray,
Whilst hollow winds through mantling ivy sigh!
And even the mouldering shrine is rent away,
Where, in his warrior weeds, the British Arthur lay.

Now look upon the sister fane of Wells!
It lifts its forehead in the summer air;
Sweet, o'er the champagne, sound its Sabbath bells,
Its roof rolls back the chant, or voice of prayer.
Anxious we ask, Will Heaven that temple spare,

Or mortal tempest sweep it from its state!
Oh! say,—shall time revere the fabric fair,
Or shall it meet, in distant years, thy fate,
Shattered, proud pile, like thee, and left as desolate!

No! to subdue or elevate the soul,
Our best, our purest feelings to refine,
Still shall the solemn diapasons roll,
Through that high fane! still hues, reflected, shine
From the tall windows on the sculptured shrine,
Tinging the pavement! for He shall afford,
He who directs the storm, his aid divine,
Because its Sion has not left thy word,
Nor sought for other guide than thee, Almighty Lord!

SILCHESTER, THE ANCIENT CALEVA

The wild pear whispers, and the ivy crawls,
Along the circuit of thine ancient walls,
Lone city of the dead! and near this mound,
The buried coins of mighty men are found,
Silent remains of Cæsars and of kings,
Soldiers of whose renown the world yet rings,
In its sad story! These have had their day
Of glory, and have passed, like sounds, away!

And such their fame! While we the spot behold,
And muse upon the tale that Time has told,
We ask where are they?—they whose clarion brayed,
Whose chariot glided, and whose war-horse neighed;
Whose cohorts hastened o'er the echoing way,
Whose eagles glittered to the orient ray!

Ask of this fragment, reared by Roman hands,
That, now, a lone and broken column stands!
Ask of that road—whose track alone remains—
That swept, of old, o'er mountains, downs, and plains;
And still along the silent champagne leads;
Where are its noise of cars and tramp of steeds?
Ask of the dead, and silence will reply;
Go, seek them in the grave of mortal vanity!

Is this a Roman veteran?—look again,—
It is a British soldier, who, in Spain,
At Albuera's glorious fight, has bled;
He, too, has spurred his charger o'er the dead!

Desolate, now—friendless and desolate—
Let him the tale of war and home relate.
His wife (and Gainsborough such a form and mien
Would paint, in harmony with such a scene),
With pensive aspect, yet demeanour bland,
A tottering infant guided by her hand,
Spoke of her own green Erin, while her child,
Amid the scene of ancient glory, smiled,
As spring's first flower smiles from a monument
Of other years, by time and ruin rent!

Lone city of the dead! thy pride is past,
Thy temples sunk, as at the whirlwind's blast!
Silent—all silent, where the mingled cries
Of gathered myriads rent the purple skies!
Here—where the summer breezes waved the wood—
The stern and silent gladiator stood,
And listened to the shouts that hailed his gushing blood.
And on this wooded mount, that oft, of yore,
Hath echoed to the Lybian lion's roar,
The ear scarce catches, from the shady glen,
The small pipe of the solitary wren.

RESTORATION OF MALMESBURY ABBEY

Monastic and time-consecrated fane!
Thou hast put on thy shapely state again,
Almost august as in thy early day,
Ere ruthless Henry rent thy pomp away.
No more the mass on holidays is sung,
The Host high raised, or fuming censer swung;
No more, in amice white, the fathers, slow,
With lighted tapers, in long order go;
Yet the tall window lifts its arched height,
As to admit heaven's pale, but purer light;
Those massy clustered columns, whose long rows,
Even at noonday, in shadowy pomp repose,
Amid the silent sanctity of death,
Like giants seem to guard the dust beneath.
Those roofs re-echo (though no altars blaze)
The prayer of penitence, the hymn of praise;
Whilst meek Religion's self, as with a smile,
Reprints the tracery of the holy pile,
Worthy its guest, the temple. What remains?
O mightiest Master! thy immortal strains
These roofs demand; listen! with prelude slow,

Solemnly sweet, yet full, the organs blow.
And, hark! again, heard ye the choral chant
Peal through the echoing arches, jubilant?
More softly now, imploring litanies,
Wafted to heaven, and mingling with the sighs
Of penitence from yon altar rise;
Again the vaulted roof "Hosannahs" rings—
"Hosannah! Lord of lords, and King of kings!"
Rent, but not prostrate; stricken, yet sublime;
Reckless alike of injuries or time;
Thou, unsubdued, in silent majesty,
The tempest hast defied and shalt defy!
The temple of our Sion so shall mock
The muttering storm, the very earthquake's shock,
Founded, O Christ, on thy eternal rock!

ON THE FUNERAL OF CHARLES THE FIRST, AT NIGHT, IN ST GEORGE'S CHAPEL, WINDSOR

The castle clock had tolled midnight:
With mattock and with spade,
And silent, by the torches' light,
His corse in earth we laid.

The coffin bore his name, that those
Of other years might know,
When earth its secrets should disclose,
Whose bones were laid below.

"Peace to the dead" no children sung,
Slow pacing up the nave,—
No prayers were read, no knell was rung,
As deep we dug his grave.

We only heard the winter's wind,
In many a sullen gust,
As, o'er the open grave inclined,
We murmured, "Dust to dust!"
A moonbeam from the arch's height
Streamed, as we placed the stone;
The long aisles started into light,
And all the windows shone.

We thought we saw the banners then,
That shook along the walls,
Whilst the sad shades of mailèd men
Were gazing on the stalls.

'Tis gone! again on tombs defaced
Sits darkness more profound;
And only by the torch we traced
The shadows on the ground.

And now the chilling, freezing air
Without blew long and loud;
Upon our knees we breathed one prayer,
Where he slept in his shroud.

We laid the broken marble floor,—
No name, no trace appears,—
And when we closed the sounding door,
We thought of him with tears.

ON SEEING PLANTS IN THE WINDOWS OF SETH WARD'S COLLEGE, ENDOWED FOR WIDOWS OF CLERGYMEN, AT SALISBURY

There is but one stage more in life's long way,
O widowed women! Sadly upon your path
Hath evening, bringing change of scenes and friends,
Descended, since the morn of hope shone fair;
And lonely age is yours, whose tears have fallen
Upon a husband's grave,—with whom, long since,
Amid the quietude of village scenes,
We walked, and saw your little children grow
Like lovely plants beside you, or adorned
Your lowly garden-plot with summer flowers;
And heard the bells, upon the Sabbath morn,
Chime to the village church, when he you loved
Walked by your side to prayer. These images
Of days long passed, of love and village life,
You never can forget; and many a plant
Green growing at the windows of your home,
And one pale primrose, in small earthen vase,
And bird-cage in the sunshine at the door,
Remember you, though in a city pent,
Of morning walks along the village lane,
Of the lark singing through the vernal hail,
Of swallows skimming o'er the garden pond,—
Remember you of children and of friends
Parted, and pleasant summers gone! 'Tis meet
To nurse such recollections, not with pain,
But in submission to the will of Heaven;
Thankful that here, as the calm eve of life,

In pious privacy, steals on, one hearth
Of charity is yours; and cold must be
That heart, which, of the changes of the world
Unmindful, could receive you but as guests,
Who had seen happier days!
Yet one stage more,
And your long rest will be with him you loved.
Oh! pray to God that each may rest in hope!

MORLEY'S FAREWELL TO THE COTTAGE OF ISAAK WALTON. TO KENNA

England, a long farewell! a long farewell,
My country, to thy woods, and streams, and hills!
Where I have heard in youth the Sabbath bell,
For many a year now mute: affection fills
Mine eyes with tears; yet resolute to wait,
Whatever ills betide, whatever fate;
Far from my native land, from sights of woe,
From scaffolds drenched in generous blood, I go.
Sad, in a land of strangers, when I bend
With grief of heart, without a home or friend,
And chiefly when with weary thoughts oppressed,
I see the sun sink slowly in the west;
Then, doubly feeling my forsaken lot,
I shall remember, far away, this cot
Of humble piety, and prayer, and peace,
And thee, dear friend, till my heart's beatings cease.
Warm from that heart I breathe one parting prayer:
My good old friend, may God Almighty spare—
Spare, for the sake of that poor child, thy life,—
Long spare it for thy meek and duteous wife.
Perhaps o'er them, when the hard storm blows loud,
We both may be at rest and in our shroud;
Or we may live to talk of these sad times,
When virtue was reviled, and direst crimes
Faith's awful name usurped. We may again
Hear heavenly truths in the time-hallowed fane,
And the full chant. Oh! if that day arrive,
And we, old friend, though bowed with age, survive,
How happy, whilst our days on earth shall last,
To pray and think of seasons that are past,
Till on our various way the night shall close,
And in one hallowed pile, at last, our bones repose.

THE GRAVE OF BISHOP KEN

On yonder heap of earth forlorn,
Where Ken his place of burial chose,
Peacefully shine, O Sabbath morn!
And, eve, with gentlest hush, repose.

To him is reared no marble tomb,
Within the dim cathedral fane;
But some faint flowers, of summer bloom,
And silent falls the wintry rain.

No village monumental stone
Records a verse, a date, a name—
What boots it? when thy task is done,
Christian, how vain the sound of fame!

Oh! far more grateful to thy God,
The voices of poor children rise,
Who hasten o'er the dewy sod,
"To pay their morning sacrifice."

And can we listen to their hymn,
Heard, haply, when the evening knell
Sounds, where the village brow is dim,
As if to bid the world farewell!

Without a thought that from the dust
The morn shall wake the sleeping clay,
And bid the faithful and the just
Upspring to heaven's eternal day!

THE LEGEND OF ST CECILIA AND THE ANGEL

'Twas when, O meekest eve! thy shadows dim
Were slowly stealing round,
With more impassioned sound
Divine Cecilia sang her vesper hymn,
And swelled the solemn chord
In hallelujahs to thy name, O Lord!
And now I see her raise
Rapt adoration's gaze,
With lips just opening, and with humid eyes
Uplifted; whilst the strain
Now sinks, now swells again;
Now rising, seems to blend with heaven's own harmonies.

But who is that, divinely fair,
With more than mortal beauty in his mien;
With eyes of heavenly hue and glistening hair,
His white and ample wings half seen!
O radiant and immortal guest!
Why hast thou left thy seraph throng,
On earth the triumph to attest
Of Beauty, Piety, and Song!

SUPPOSED ADDRESS TO BISHOP KEN

Though his words might well deceive me,
Though to earth abased I bend,
Christian guide, thou wilt not leave me,
Thus on earth without a friend!

I thought his vows were oaths in heaven,
Nor dare I here my fault deny;
For all my soul to him was given,
God knows how true, how tenderly!

Though wronged and desolate and dying,
His pride, his coldness, I forgot,
And fell upon his bosom, crying,
Forsake me not—forsake me not!

I left my father, and my mother,
Whom I no more on earth may see,
But I have found a father, brother,
And more than every friend, in thee!

Although his words might well deceive me,
Though wronged, and desolate I lie,
Christian guide, thou wilt not leave me,
Oh, teach me to repent and die!

ON AN ECLIPSE OF THE MOON AT MIDNIGHT

Up, up, into the vast extended space,
Thou art ascending in thy majesty,
Beautiful moon, the queen of the pale sky!
But what is that which gathers on thy face,
A dark mysterious shade, eclipsing, slow,
The splendour of thy calm and steadfast light?

It is the shadow of this world of woe,
Of this vast moving world; portentous sight!
As if we almost stood and saw more near
Its very action—almost heard it roll
On, in the swiftness of its dread career,
As it hath rolled for ages! Hush, my soul!
Listen! there is no sound; but we could hear
The murmur of its multitudes, who toil
Through their brief hour. The heart might well recoil;
But this is ever sounding in His ear
Who made it, and who said, "Let there be light!"
And we, the creatures of a mortal hour,
'Mid hosts of worlds, are ever in his sight,
Catching, as now, dim glimpses of his power.
The time shall come when all this mighty scene
Darkness shall wrap, as it had never been.
O Father of all worlds! be thou our guide,
And lead us gently on, from youth to age,
Through the dark valley of our pilgrimage;
Enough if thus, bending to thy high will,
We hold our Christian course through good or ill,
And to the end with faith and hope abide.

TO LADY VALLETORT, ON HEARING HER SING "GLORIA IN EXCELSIS," WITH THREE OTHER YOUNG LADIES, AT LACOCK ABBEY, OCTOBER

Fair inmate of these ivied walls, beneath
Whose silent cloisters Ella sleeps in death,
Let loftier bards, in rich and glowing lays,
Thy gentleness, thy grace, thy virtue praise!
Be mine to breathe one prayer; when all rejoice,
One parting prayer, still mindful of that voice,
And musing on the sacred song which stole,
Sweet as the spell of peace, upon the soul;
In those same scenes, where once the chapel dim
Echoed the cloistered sisters' vesper hymn:—
Live long! live happy! tranquil through the strife
And the loud stir of this tumultuous life!
Live long, live happy! and when many a day
Hath passed in the heart's harmony away;
When Eve's pale hand the gates of life shall close,
And hush the landscape to its last repose;
May sister seraphs meet with welcome song,
And gently say, Why have you stayed so long?

ON SEEING A BUST OF R. B. SHERIDAN, FROM A CAST TAKEN AFTER DEATH

Alas, poor Sheridan! when first we met,
'Twas 'mid a smiling circle, and thine eye,
That flashed with eloquent hilarity
And playful fancy, I remember yet
Freshly as yesterday. The gay and fair,
The young and beautiful,—now in their graves—
Surrounded us; while on the lucid wave
Of Hampton's waters, to the morning air
The streamer softly played of our light boat,
Which seemed as on a magic sea to float.

I saw thee after in this crowd of life,
Conflicting, but yet blandly, with its strife.
As the still car of Time rolled on, thy cheek
Wore the same smile, yet with a trace more weak.
Lone sorrow came as life declined, and care,
And age, with slowly furrowing line, was there.

I could have spared this fearful sight! Most strange
Is the eventful tale of mortal change,
Inevitable; but death, brought so nigh,
In form so tangible, harrows the eye.
As all the past floats like a cloud away,
Alas, poor Sheridan! I turn and say,
Not without feelings which such sights impart,
Sad, but instructive, to the Christian's heart!

May.

RETURN OF GEORGE III. TO WINDSOR CASTLE

Not that thy name, illustrious dome! recalls
The pomp of chivalry in bannered halls,
The blaze of beauty, and the gorgeous sights
Of heralds, trophies, steeds, and crested knights;
Not that young Surrey there beguiled the hour
With "eyes upturned unto the maiden's tower;"
Oh! not for these the muse officious brings
Her gratulations to the best of kings;
But that from cities and from crowds withdrawn,
Calm peace may meet him on the twilight lawn;
That here among these gray primeval trees,
He may inhale health's animating breeze;

That these old oaks, which far their shadows cast,
May soothe him while they whisper of the past;
And when from that proud terrace he surveys
Slow Thames devolving his majestic maze
(Now lost on the horizon's verge, now seen
Winding through lawns and woods, and pastures green),
May he reflect upon the waves that roll,
Bearing a nation's wealth from pole to pole;
And own (ambition's proudest boast above)
A king's best glory is his country's love.

ON MEETING SOME FRIENDS OF YOUTH AT CHELTENHAM, FOR THE FIRST TIME SINCE WE PARTED AT OXFORD

"And wept to see the paths of life divide."—Shenstone.

Here the companions of our careless prime,
Whom fortune's various ways have severed long,
Since that fair dawn when Hope her vernal song
Sang blithe, with features marked by stealing time
At these restoring springs are met again!
We, young adventurers on life's opening road,
Set out together; to their last abode
Some have sunk silent, some a while remain,
Some are dispersed; of many, growing old
In life's obscurer bourne, no tale is told.
Here, ere the shades of the long night descend,
And all our wanderings in oblivion end,
The parted meet once more, and pensive trace
(Marked by that hand unseen, whose iron pen
Writes "mortal change" upon the fronts of men)
The creeping furrows in each other's face.
Where shall we meet again? Reflection sighs;
Where? In the dust! Time rushing on replies:
Then hail the hope that lights the pilgrim's way,
Where there is neither change, nor darkness, nor decay!

THE LAY OF TALBOT, THE TROUBADOUR. A LEGEND OF LACOCK ABBEY

PART FIRST

At Rouen Richard kept his state,
Released from captive thrall;
And girt with many a warrior guest

He feasted in the hall!

The rich metheglin mantled high,
The wine was berry red,
When tidings came that Salisbury,
His early friend, was dead;

And that his sole surviving child,
The heiress of his wealth,
By crafty kinsmen and allies
Was borne away by stealth;

Was borne away from Normandy,
Where, secretly confined,
She heard no voice of those she loved,
But sighed to the north wind.

Haply from some lone castle's tower
Or solitary strand,
Even now she gazes o'er the deep,
That laves her father's land!

King Richard cries, My minstrel knights,
Who will the task achieve,
To seek through France and Normandy
The orphan left to grieve?

Young William Talbot then did speak,
Betide me weal or woe,
From Michael's castle through the land
A pilgrim I will go.

He clad him in his pilgrim weeds,
With trusty staff in hand,
And scallop shell, and took his way,
A wanderer through the land.

For two long years he journeyed on,
A pilgrim, day by day,
Through many a forest dark and drear,
By many a castle gray.

At length, when one clear morn of frost
Was shining on the main,
Forth issuing from a castle gate
He saw a female train!

With lightsome step and waving hair,

Before them ran a child,
And gathering from the sands a shell,
Ran back to them, and smiled.

Himself unseen among the rocks,
He saw her point her hand;
And cry, I would go home, go home,
To my poor father's land.

The bell tolled from the turret gray,
Cold freezing fell the dew,
To the portcullis hastening back
The female train withdrew.

Those turrets and the battlements,
Time and the storm had beat,
And sullenly the ocean tide
Came rolling at his feet.

Young Talbot cast away his staff,
The harp is in his hand,
A minstrel at the castle gate,
A porter saw him stand.

And who art thou, the porter cried,
Young troubadour, now say,
For welcome in the castle hall
Will be to-night thy lay;

For this the birthday is of one,
Whose father now is cold;
An English maiden, rich in fee,
And this year twelve years old.

I love, myself, now growing old,
To hear the wild harp's sound:
But whence, young harper, dost thou come,
And whither art thou bound?

Though I am young, the harper said,
From Syria's sands I come,
A minstrel warrior of the Cross,
Now poor and wandering home.

And I can tell of mighty deeds,
By bold King Richard done,
King Richard of "the Lion's heart,"
Foes quail to look upon.

Then lead me to the castle hall,
And let the fire be bright,
For never hall nor bower hath heard
A lay like mine to-night.

The windows gleam within the hall,
The fire is blazing bright,
And the young harper's hair and harp
Are shining in the light.

Fair dames and warriors clad in steel
Now gather round to hear,
And oft that little maiden's eyes
Are glistening with a tear.

For, when the minstrel sang of wars,
At times, with softer sound,
He touched the chords, as mourning those
Now laid in the cold ground.

He sang how brave King Richard pined
In a dark tower immured,
And of the long and weary nights,
A captive, he endured.

The faithful Blondel to his harp
One song began to sing;
It ceased; the king takes up the strain;
It is his lord and king!

Of Sarum then, and Sarum's plain,
That poor child heard him speak,
When the first tear-drop in her eye
Fell silent on her cheek.

For, as the minstrel told his tale,
The breathless orphan maid
Thought of the land where, in the grave,
Her father's bones were laid.

Hush, hush! the winds are piping loud,
The midnight hour is sped,
The hours of morn are stealing fast,
Harper, to bed! to bed!

PART SECOND

The two long years had passed away,
When castle Galliard rose,
As built at once by elfin hands,
And scorning time or foes.

It might be thought that Merlin's imps
Were tasked to raise the wall,
That unheard axes fell the woods,
While unseen hammers fall.

As hung by magic on a rock,
The castle-keep looked down
O'er rocks and rivers, and the smoke
Of many a far off town.

And now, young knights and minstrels gay
Obeyed their masters' call,
And loud rejoicing held the feast
In the new raftered hall.

His minstrels and his mailed peers
Were seated at the board,
And at his side the highest sat
William of the Long Sword.

This youthful knight, of princely birth,
Was dazzling to behold,
For his chain-mail from head to foot
All glistened o'er with gold.

His surcoat dyed with azure blue
In graceful foldings hung,
And there the golden lions ramped,
With bloody claws and tongue.

With crimson belt around his waist
His sword was girded on;
The hilt, a cross to kiss in death,
Radiant with jewels shone.

The names and banners of each knight
It were too long to tell;
Here sat the brave Montgomery,
There Bertrand and Rozell.

Of Richard's unresisted sword

A noble minstrel sung,
Whilst to an hundred answering harps
The blazing gallery rung.

So all within was merriment—
When, suddenly, a shout,
As of some unexpected guest,
Burst from the crowd without.

Now not a sound, and scarce a breath,
Through the long hall is heard,
When, with a young maid by his side,
A vizored knight appeared.

Up the long hall they held their way,
On to the royal seat;
Then both together, hand in hand,
Knelt at King Richard's feet.

Talbot, a Talbot! rang the hall
With gratulation wild,
Long live brave Talbot, and long live
Earl William's new found child!

Amid a scene so new and strange,
This poor maid could not speak;
King Richard took her by the hand,
And gently kissed her cheek;

Then placed her, smiling through a tear,
By his brave brother's side:
Long live brave Longspe! rang the hall,
Long live his future bride!

To noble Richard, this fair child,
His ward, was thus restored;
Destined to be the future bride
Of Him of the Long Sword.

THE ARK: A POEM FOR MUSIC.

MICHAEL, ARCHANGEL
High on Imaus' solitary van,
Which overlooked the kingdoms of the world,
With stature more majestic, his stern brow
In the clear light, the thunder at his feet;

In his right hand the flaming sword that waved
O'er Eden's gate; and in his left the trump,
That on the day of doom shall sound and wake
Earth's myriads, starting from the wormy grave,
The great archangel stood: and, hark, his voice!

AIR
It comes, it comes, o'er cities, temples, towers;
O'er mountain heights I see the deluge sweep;
Heard ye from earth the cry at that last hour?
Heard ye the tossing of the desert deep?
How dismal is its roar!
I heard the sound of multitudes no more.
Great Lord of heaven and earth, thy voice is fate;
Thou canst destroy, as first thou didst create!

He stood and sounded the archangel's trump;
And now a choir of seraphim drew near,
By Raphael led: in sad and solemn strains,
They raised their supplication to Heaven's throne.

CHORUS
O Thou whose mighty voice, "Let there be light!"
Dread Chaos heard, when the great sun from night
Burst forth, and demon shadows fled away,
And the green earth sprang beautiful to day!
Oh! merciful in judgment, hear our prayer;
Behold the world which Thou hast made so fair,
And man the mourner, man the sinner, spare.

GABRIEL (RECITATIVE)
Oh! what a change have sin and sorrow made!
In the beginning, God created heaven
And earth; and man, amid the works of God,
Majestic stood, his noblest creature, formed
In God's own image; and his fair abode
Was visited by seraph shapes of light,
And sin and death were not.

TRIO
Mourn, mourn, ye bowers
Of paradise, ye pleasant hills and woods!
Mourn; for the dreadful voice hath passed that shrunk
Your streams, and withered all your blooming flowers.
And thou, created in God's image, man!
Go forth into the nether world; "for dust
Thou art, and unto dust shalt thou return."

RECITATIVE
So, led by Sin and Death, and his pale troop,
Impatient came, and all this goodly scene,
As at the withering of a demon's curse, was blasted.
Then they two went forth, from whom
Their children sorrow and sin and death derived:
They two went forth into the forlorn world,
Heart-struck, but not despairing.
From that hour
Death's shadow walks on earth, a hideous form,
Saddening the very sun; and giant crimes
Have multiplied, till to the throne of God,
And the serene air of untroubled bliss,
The noise of violence, and the cries of blood,
Have from the ground ascended.
Therefore God
Me hath commissioned to uplift the trump
Of doom, and sweep this world of sin away!

WRITTEN AFTER THE CONSECRATION OF THE NEW CHURCH AT KINGSWOOD

When first the fane, that, white, on Kingswood-Pen,
Arrests, far off, the pausing stranger's ken,
Echoed the hymn of praise, and on that day,
Which seemed to shine with more auspicious ray,
When thousands listened to the prelate there,
Who called on God, with consecrating prayer;—
I saw a village-maid, almost a child,
Even as a light-haired cherub, undefiled
From earth's rank fume, with innocent look, her eye
Meekly uplifted to the throne on high,
Join in the full choir's solemn harmony.
Oh, then, how many boding thoughts arose,
Lest, long ere varied life's uncertain close,
Those looks of modesty, that open truth
Lighting the forehead of ingenuous youth—
Lest these, as slowly steal maturing years,
Should fade, and grief succeed, and dimming tears;
Then should the cheek be blanched with early care,
Sin mark its first and furrowing traces there,
With touch corroding mar the altered mien,
And leave a canker where the rose had been;
Then the sweet child, whose smiles can now impart
Joy overpowering to a mother's heart,
Might bring down, when not anxious love could save,
That mother's few gray hairs with sorrow to the grave!

But, hark! the preacher's voice, his accents bland,
Behold his kindled look, his lifted hand;
What holy fervour wakes at his command!
He speaks of faith, of mercy from above,
Of heavenly hope, of a Redeemer's love!
Hence every thought, but that which shows fair youth
Advancing in the paths of peace and truth!
Which shows thy light, O pure religion! shed,
Like a faint glory, on a daughter's head,
Who shall each parent's love, through life, repay,
And add a transport to their dying day!
I saw an old man, on his staff reclined,
Who seemed to every human change resigned:—
He, with white locks, and long-descending beard,
A patriarch of other years appeared:
And thine, O aged, solitary man!
Was life's enchanted way, when life began,
The sunshine on each mountain, and the strain
Of some sweet melody, in every plain;
Thine was illusive fortune's transient gleam,
And young love's broken, but delicious dream;
Those mocking visions of thy youth are flown,
And thou dost bend on death's dark brink alone
The light associates of thy vernal day,
Where are they? Blown, like the sere leaves, away;
And thou dost seem a trunk, on whose bare head
The gray moss of uncounted days is spread!
I know thee not, old man! yet traits like these,
Upon thy time-worn features fancy sees.
Another, or another year, for thee,
Haply, "the silver cord shall loosed be!"
Then listen, whilst warm eloquence portrays
That "better country" to thy anxious gaze,
Who art a weary, way-worn "pilgrim here,"
And soon from life's vain masque to disappear.
O aged man! lift up thine eyes—behold
What brighter views of distant light unfold;
What though the loss of strength thou dost deplore,
Or broken loves, or friends that are no more?
What though gay youth no more his song renews,
And summer-light dies, like the rainbow hues?
The Christian hails the ray that cheers the gloom,
And throws its heavenly halo round the tomb.
Who bade the grave its mouldering vault unclose?
"Christ—Christ who died; yea, rather, Christ who rose!"
Hope lifts from earth her tear-illumined eye,
She sees, dispersed, the world's last tempest fly;
Sees death, arrested 'mid his havoc vast,

Lord, at thy feet his broken weapons cast!
In circles, far retiring from the sight,
Till, undistinguished, they are lost in light,
Admiring seraphim suspend their wings,
Whilst, hark! the eternal empyrean rings,
Hosannah, Lord of lords, and King of kings!
Such thoughts arose, when from the crowded fane
I saw retire the mute, assembled train;
Their images beguiled my homeward way,
Which high o'er Lansdowne's lonely summit lay.
There seemed a music in the evening gale,
And looking back on the long-spreading vale,
Methought a blessing waited on the hour,
As the last light from heaven shone on the distant tower.

ON THE DEATH OF DR BURGESS, THE LATE BISHOP OF SALISBURY

Sainted old man, for more than eighty years,
Thee—tranquilly and stilly-creeping—age,
Led to the confines of the sepulchre,
And thy last day on earth—but "Father—Lord—
Which art in heaven"—how pure a faith, and heart
Unmoved, amid the changes of this life,
And tumult of the world,—and oh! what hope,—
What love and constancy of the calm mind,
And tears to misery from the inmost heart
Flowing—at times, a brief sweet smile and voice
How bland, and studies, various and profound,
Of learned languages—but, ever first,
That learning which the oracles of God
Unfolds, even to the close of life's long day
Thy course accompanies!
But, thou, farewell,
And live—this mortal veil removed—in bliss;
Live with the saints in light, whom Christ had loved.
But pardon us, left in this vale of tears,
For one last tear upon thy cold remains—
Pardon, beloved and venerated shade!

LINES WRITTEN ON FONTHILL ABBEY

The mighty master waved his wand, and, lo!
On the astonished eye the glorious show
Burst like a vision! Spirit of the place!

Has the Arabian wizard with his mace
Smitten the barren downs, far onward spread,
And bade the enchanted palace rise instead?
Bade the dark woods their solemn shades extend,
High to the clouds yon spiry tower ascend?
And starting from the umbrageous avenue
Spread the rich pile, magnificent to view?
Enter! From the arched portal look again,
Back on the lessening woods and distant plain!
Ascend the steps! The high and fretted roof
Is woven by some elfin hand aloof;
Whilst from the painted windows' long array
A mellow light is shed as not of day.
How gorgeous all! Oh, never may the spell
Be broken, that arrayed those radiant forms so well!

EPITAPH ON BENJAMIN TREMLYN, AN OLD SOLDIER, BURIED IN BREMHILL CHURCHYARD AT THE AGE OF—.

A poor old soldier shall not lie unknown,
Without a verse, and this recording stone.
'Twas his in youth o'er distant lands to stray,
Danger and death companions of his way.
Here in his native village, drooping, age
Closed the lone evening of his pilgrimage.
Speak of the past, of names of high renown,
Or his brave comrades long to dust gone down,
His eye with instant animation glowed,
Though ninety winters on his head had snowed.
His country, whilst he lived, a boon supplied,
And faith her shield held o'er him when he died;
Hope, Christian, that his spirit lives with God,
And pluck the wild weeds from his lowly sod,
Where, dust to dust, beside the chancel's shade,
Till the last trumpet sounds, a brave man's bones are laid.

EPITAPH ON ROBERT SOUTHEY

Christian! for none who scorns that holy name
Can gaze with honest eyes on Southey's fame;
Christian! bow down thy head in humble fear,
And think what God-given powers lie silenced here:
Wit, judgment, memory, patience unsubdued,
Conception vast, and pious fortitude.

Learning possessed no steeps, and truth no shore,
Beyond his step to tread, his wing to soar;
His was the historian's pen, the poet's lyre,
The churchman's ardour, and the patriot's fire;
While fireside charities, Heaven's gentlest dower,
Lent genius all their warmth and all their power.
O Church and State of England! thine was he
In living fame, thine be his memory!
Thou saw'st him live, in faith expire,
Go, bid thy sons to follow, and admire!

SONNET. WRITTEN IN A COPY OF FALCONER'S "SHIPWRECK"

What pale and bleeding youth, whilst the fell blast
Howls o'er the wreck, and fainter sinks the cry
Of struggling wretches ere, o'erwhelmed, they die,
Yet floats upborne upon the driving mast!
O poor Arion! has thy sweetest strain,
That charmed old ocean's wildest solitude,
At this dread hour his waves' dark might subdued!
Let sea-maids thy reclining head sustain,
And wipe the blood and briny drops that soil
Thy features; give once more the wreathed shell
To ring with melody! Ah, fruitless toil!
O'er thy devoted head the tempests swell,
More loud relentless ocean claims his spoil:
Peace! and may weeping sea-maids sing thy knell!

ON FIRST HEARING CARADORI SING

Spirit of beauty, and of heavenly song!
No longer seek in vain, 'mid the loud throng,
'Mid the discordant tumults of mankind,
One spirit, gentle as thyself, to find.

Oh! listen, and suspend thy upward wings,
Listen—for, hark! 'tis Caradori sings;
Hear, on the cadence of each thrilling note,
Airs scarce of earth, and sounds seraphic float!

See, in the radiant smile that lights her face;
See, in that form, a more than magic grace;
And say (repaid for every labour past)
Beautiful spirit, thou art found at last!

SALISBURY CATHEDRAL

Here stood the city of the dead; look round—
Dost thou not mark a visionary band,
Druids and bards upon the summits stand,
Of the majestic and time-hallowed mound?
Hark! heard ye not at times the acclaiming word
Of harps, as when those bards, in white array,
Hailed the ascending lord of light and day!
Here, o'er the clouds, the first cathedral rose,
Whose prelates now in yonder fane repose,
Among the mighty of years passed away;
For there her latest seat Religion chose,
There still to heaven ascends the holy lay,
And never may those shrines in dust and silence close!

April.

LOCKSWELL

Pure fount, that, welling from this wooded hill,
Dost wander forth, as into life's wide vale,
Thou to the traveller dost tell no tale
Of other years; a lone, unnoticed rill,
In thy forsaken track, unheard of men,
Melting thy own sweet music through the glen.
Time was when other sounds and songs arose;
When o'er the pensive scene, at evening's close,
The distant bell was heard; or the full chant,
At morn, came sounding high and jubilant;
Or, stealing on the wildered pilgrim's way,
The moonlight "Miserere" died away,
Like all things earthly.
Stranger, mark the spot;
No echoes of the chiding world intrude.
The structure rose and vanished; solitude
Possessed the woods again; old Time forgot,
Passing to wider spoil, its place and name.
Since then, even as the clouds of yesterday,
Seven hundred years have well-nigh passed away;
No wreck remains of all its early pride;
Like its own orisons, its fame has died.
But this pure fount, through rolling years the same,

Yet lifts its small still voice, like penitence,
Or lowly prayer. Then pass admonished hence,
Happy, thrice happy, if, through good or ill,
Christian, thy heart respond to this forsaken rill.

ON MOZART

Oh! still, as with a seraph's voice, prolong
The harmonies of that enchanting song,
Till, listening, we might almost think we hear,
Beyond this cloudy world, in the pure sphere
Of light, acclaiming hosts the throne surrounding,
The long hosannahs evermore resounding,
Soft voices interposed in pure accord,
Breathing a holier charm. Oh! every word
Falls like a drop of silver, as the strain,
In winding sweetness, swells and sinks again.
Sing ever thus, beguiling life's long way,
As here, poor pilgrims of the earth, we stray;
And, lady, when thy pilgrimage shall end,
And late the shades of the long night descend,
May sister seraphs welcome with a song,
And gently say, Why have you stayed so long?

EPITAPH ON JOHN HARDING, IN THE CHURCHYARD OF BREMHILL

Lay down thy pilgrim staff upon this heap,
And till the morning of redemption sleep,
Old wayfarer of earth! From youth to age,
Long, but not weary, was thy pilgrimage,
Thy Christian pilgrimage; for faith and prayer
Alone enabled thee some griefs to bear.
Lone, in old age, without a husband's aid,
Thy wife shall pray beside thee to be laid;
For more than a kind father didst thou prove
To fourteen children of her faithful love.
May future fathers of the village trace
The same sure path to the same resting-place;
And future sons, taught in their strength to save,
Learn their first lesson from a poor man's grave!

April .

ON THE DEATH OF WILLIAM LINLEY, ESQ., THE COMPOSER OF THE MUSIC OF "THE DUENNA," ETC

Poor Linley! I shall miss thee sadly, now
Thou art not in the world; for few remain
Who loved like thee the high and holy strain
Of harmony's immortal master.
Thou
Didst honour him; and none I know, who live,
Could even a shadow, a faint image give,
With chord and voice, of those rich harmonies,
Which, mingled in one mighty volume, rise,
Glorious, from earth to heaven, so to express
Choral acclaim to Heaven's almightiness,
As thou! Therefore, amid the world's deep roar,
When the sweet visions of young Hope are fled,
And many friends dispersed, and many dead,
I grieve that I shall hear that voice no more.

INSCRIBED TO THE MARCHIONESS OF LANSDOWNE

Go to assemblies of the rich and gay,
The blazing hall of grandeur, and the throng
Of cities, and there listen to the song
Of festive harmony; then pause, and say,
Where is she found, who in her sphere might shine,
Attracting all? Where is she found, whose place
And dignity the proudest court might grace?
Go, where the desolate and dying pine
On their cold bed; open the cottage door;
Ask of that aged pair, who feebly bend
O'er their small evening fire, who is their friend;
Ask of these children of the village poor;
For this, at the great judgment, thou shalt find
Heaven's mercy, Lady, merciful and kind.

HYMN FOR MUSIC, AFTER THE BATTLE OF WATERLOO

Perish! Almighty Justice cried,
And struck the avenging blow,
And Europe shouts from side to side,
The tyrant is laid low!
Said not his heart, More blood shall stream
Around my sovereign throne?

He wakes from dire ambition's dream,
Pale, trembling, and alone.

ARIA WITH CHORUS
Triumph! the rescued nations cry,
Triumph! ten thousand hearts reply.

Sad mother, weep no more thy children slain;
The trumpets and the battle clangours cease:
Uplift to heaven the loud, the grateful strain,
And hail the dawn of Freedom and of Peace.

CHORUS
Triumph! the rescued nations cry,
Triumph! ten thousand hearts reply.

ARIA
For joy returned, for peace restored,
Lord of all worlds, to thee we raise,
While Slaughter drops his weary sword,
To thee the hymn of gratitude and praise.

CHORUS
Triumph! the rescued nations cry,
Triumph! ten thousand hearts reply.

INSCRIPTIONS IN THE GARDENS OF BREMHILL RECTORY

ON A TREE COMMANDING A VIEW OF THE WHOLE EXTENT OF BOWOOD

When in thy sight another's vast domain
Spreads its long line of woods, dost thou complain?
Nay, rather thank the God that placed thy state
Above the lowly, but beneath the great!
And still His name with gratitude revere,
Who blessed the Sabbath of thy leisure here.

ON A RURAL SEAT

Rest, stranger, in this decorated scene,
That hangs its beds of flowers, its slopes so green;
So from the walks of life the weeds remove,
But fix thy better hopes on scenes above.

ON THE FRONT OF A HERMITAGE, NEAR A DIAL

To mark life's few and fleeting hours
I placed the dial 'midst the flowers,
Which one by one came forth and died,
Still withering by its ancient side.
Mortals, let the sight impart
Its pensive moral to thy heart!

QUIETI ET MUSIS

Be thine Retirement's peaceful joys,
And a life that makes no noise;
Save when Fancy, musing long,
Wakes her desultory song;
Sounding to the vacant ear,
Like the rill that murmurs near.

William Lisle Bowles – A Short Biography

William Lisle Bowles was born on 24th September 1762 at King's Sutton in Northamptonshire.

His great-grandfather, grandfather and his father, William Thomas Bowles, had all been parish priests and inevitably Bowles would join their line.

At the age of 14 he entered Winchester College, where the headmaster was Dr Joseph Warton (a minor poet, his most notable piece is The Enthusiast, 1744. In 1755, he taught at Winchester and from 1766 to 1793 was headmaster. His career as a critic was illustrious. He produced editions of poets such as Virgil as well as several English poets).

In 1789 Bowles published, a small quarto volume, Fourteen Sonnets, which was received with extraordinary praise, not only by the general public, but by such revered poets as Samuel Taylor Coleridge and Wordsworth.

The Sonnets were a return to an older and purer poetic style, and by their grace of expression, lyrical versification, tender tone of feeling and vivid appreciation of the wonder and beauty of nature, stood out in marked contrast to the elaborate works which then formed the bulk of English poetry.

Bowles said "Poetic trifles from solitary rambles whilst chewing the cud of sweet and bitter fancy, written from memory, confined to fourteen lines, this seemed best adapted to the unity of sentiment, the verse flowed in unpremeditated harmony as my ear directed but are far from being mere elegiac couplets".

The young Samuel Taylor Coleridge felt obliged to record his debt of gratitude to Bowles: "My obligations to Mr. Bowles were indeed important, and for radical good. At a very premature age, ... I had bewildered myself in metaphysicks, and in theological controversy. Nothing else pleased me. Poetry ... became insipid to me.... This preposterous pursuit was, beyond doubt, injurious both to my natural powers, and to the progress of my education.... But from this I was auspiciously withdrawn, chiefly by the genial influence of a style of poetry, so tender and yet so manly, so natural and real, and yet so dignified and harmonious, as the sonnets &c. of Mr. Bowles!"

In 1781 Bowles left as captain of Winchester school, and proceeded to Trinity College, Oxford, after winning a scholarship. Two years later he won the Chancellor's prize for Latin verse. It was now evident that the Church and poetry were to be his two callings.

After receiving his degree at Oxford, Bowles now began his career in service to the Church of England. In 1792, after serving as curate in Donhead St Andrew, Bowles was appointed vicar of Chicklade in Wiltshire.

Five years later, in 1797, he received the vicarage of Dumbleton in Gloucestershire, and in 1804 became vicar of Bremhill in Wiltshire, where he wrote the poem seen on Maud Heath's statue. In the same year his bishop, John Douglas, collated him to a prebendal stall in Salisbury Cathedral.

In 1818 Bowles was made chaplain to the Prince Regent, and in 1828 he was elected residentiary canon of Salisbury.

His years of service perhaps diminished both his stature as a poet and certainly the way he was viewed. For much of his career Bowles was seen as rather soft when set against his contemporaries but in the end his ability as a poet was enshrined, after a long and ferocious attack against him, by the principles he so eloquently wrote about and adhered too.

It is as well to remember that when critics suggest that compared to other poets his longer works were not to the standard that the competition achieved, that this era is perhaps without poetic equal. Set against Byron, Shelley, Keats, Wordsworth and other great luminaries of the era it is perhaps difficult to see his works in isolation for their own value.

The longer poems published by Bowles are distinguished by purity of imagination, cultured and graceful diction, and a great thoughtfulness of feeling. Among them were The Spirit of Discovery (1804), which alas was so mercilessly ridiculed by Byron; The Missionary (1813); The Grave of the Last Saxon (1822); and St John in Patmos (1833).

In 1806 he published an edition of Alexander Pope's works with notes and an essay, in which he laid down certain canons as to poetic imagery which, subject to some modification, were later accepted, but received at the time with strong opposition by admirers of Pope.

Bowles restated his views in 1819, in The Invariable Principles of Poetry. The controversy brought into sharp contrast the opposing views of poetry, which may be thought of as being either the natural or the artificial.

In personality and nature Bowles was said to be an amiable, absent-minded, but rather eccentric man. His poems speak warmly of a refinement of feeling, tenderness, and pensive thought, but are lacking in power and passion. But that should not diminish their value or appreciation to us.

Bowles maintained that images drawn from nature are poetically finer than those drawn from art; and that in the highest kinds of poetry the themes or passions handled should be of the general or elemental kind, and not the transient manners of any society. These positions were attacked by Byron, Thomas Campbell, William Roscoe and others, and for a time Bowles had to fight his corner on his own. Soon however, William Hazlitt and the Blackwood critics came to his assistance, and on the whole Bowles had reason to congratulate himself on having established certain principles which might serve as the basis of a true method of poetical criticism, and of having inaugurated, both by precept and by example, a new era in English poetry.

As well as his poetry Bowles was also responsible for writing a Life of Bishop Ken (in two volumes, 1830–1831), Coombe Ellen and St. Michael's Mount (1798), The Battle of the Nile (1799), and The Sorrows of Switzerland (1801).

Bowles also enjoyed considerable reputation as an antiquary and his principal work in that field was Hermes Britannicus (1828).

William Lisle Bowles died on April 7th, 1850 at the age of 87.

www.ingramcontent.com/pod-product-compliance
Lightning Source LLC
Chambersburg PA
CBHW061517040426
42450CB00008B/1655